THE ART OF PUBLIC SPEAKING

THE ART OF
PUBLIC SPEAKING

BY

ALBERT J. BEVERIDGE

INTRODUCTION BY D. N. DIEDRICH

NASH PUBLISHING
LOS ANGELES

Library of Congress Catalog Card Number: 73-92961
International Standard Book Number: 0-8402-8078-5

Published simultaneously in the United States and Canada
by Nash Publishing Corporation, 9255 Sunset Boulevard,
Los Angeles, California 90069

Printed in the United States of America

Nash First Printing

INTRODUCTION

A nation's oratory echoes the hopes, dreams, aspirations, struggles, despair, and triumphs of its people. Albert Jeremiah Beveridge (October 6, 1862-April 27, 1927) was a significant contributor to America's eloquence, and his advocacy included: Americanism, moral and ethical standards, progressivism, and expansion of the Republic. He favored reciprocal trade agreements, the direct primary, popular election of senators, conservation of natural resources, a permanent nonpartisan tariff commission, active pursuit of new markets abroad, legislation to end the exploitation of child labor, and a meat-inspection law— the forerunner of our pure food and drug legislation. Beveridge spoke of America's destiny and was determined to achieve his.

He distinguished himself as a lawyer, a U.S. senator from Indiana between 1899 and 1911, and as the recipient of a 1920

Pulitzer Prize for his four-volume biography of Chief Justice Marshall.

Beveridge was frequently discussed as a potential Republican presidential or vice-presidential candidate. He helped establish the Progressive party, keynoted its first national convention, and was its candidate for governor of Indiana. Public address and scholarship were taproots of his career.

Meticulous research and preparation were standards of his speeches. They were logical and clear in their structure, argumentation, and supporting materials, and were presented with seriousness of purpose and without digressions.

Critics have carefully documented his style of speaking and its transition. His earliest efforts reflected the influence of the artificiality frequently identified with speech contests—many of which he won as a college student. The speeches tended to impress the eye and ear, rather than to present the direct expression of an idea. Even Beveridge referred to them as "great cheers" or "touch-to-tears" speeches. They were labeled "word symphonies," and Mr. Dooley, the creation of philosophical American humorist Finley Peter Dunne, said one of them was "a speech ye cud waltz to."

The transition is demonstrated in the following sentences from his keynote address to the National Progressive Convention in 1912:

> We stand for a nobler America. We stand for an undivided Nation. We stand for a broader liberty, a fuller justice. We stand for social brotherhood as against savage individualism. We stand for an intelligent cooperation instead of a reckless competition. We stand for mutual helpfulness instead of mutual hatred. We stand for equal rights as a fact of life instead of a catchword of politics. We stand for the rule of the people as a practical truth instead of a meaningless pretense. We stand for a representative government that represents the people. We battle for the actual rights of man.
>
> We found a party through which all who believe with us can work with us;

or rather, we declare our allegiance to a party which the people themselves have founded.

For this party comes from the grass roots. It has grown from the soil of the people's hard necessities. It has the vitality of the people's strong convictions. The people have work to be done, and our party is here to do that work. . . .

Albert J. Beveridge summarized what experience had taught him concerning public speaking in an article that first appeared in the April 26, 1924, issue of the *Saturday Evening Post* and, subsequently, in the form presented here. *The Art of Public Speaking* does not fetter us with complicated rules written by one who is removed from the practical questions. It is instruction by a successful practitioner of the art. The rules are few, but the lessons and advice are unmistakable and contemporary.

Beveridge considers the public speaker to be a teacher and counselor who possesses sincerity of purpose and intellectual integrity. The speaker has studied, reflected, and reacted to the ideas presented. Comprehensive reading and detailed preparation are mandatory. Careful rewriting and condensation of the speech aid in the lucidity and logical progression of ideas. Anticipate and then observe the audience for reactions of understanding.

These excerpts from a speech delivered in 1898 underscore his early style. The popular response to the address, however, brought him national prominence and, in 1899, he ·was selected as U.S. senator by the Indiana General Assembly.

In 1789 the flag of the Republic waved over 4,000,000 souls in thirteen states, and their savage territory which stretched to the Mississippi, to Canada, to the Floridas. The timid minds of that day said that no new territory was needed, and, for the hour, they were right. But Jefferson, through whose intellect the centuries marched; Jefferson, who dreamed of Cuba as an American state; Jefferson, the first Imperialist of the Republic— Jefferson acquired that imperial territory which swept from the Mississippi to the mountains, from Texas to the British possessions, and the march of the flag began! The infidels to the gospel of liberty raved, but the flag swept on! . . . Those who deny the power of free institutions to expand urged every argument, and more, that we hear, today; but the people's judgment approved the command of their blood, and the march of the flag went on! . . . The Cassandras prophesied every prophecy of despair we hear, today, but the march of the flag went on! . . . And now, obeying the same voice that Jefferson heard and obeyed, that Grant heard and obeyed, that Harrison heard and obeyed, our President today plants the flag over all the islands of the seas, outposts of commerce, citadels of national security, and the march of the flag goes on! . . .

The oratorical furniture and horticulture contained in this passage are certainly excessive. However, as Beveridge became more sensitive to his audiences and studied their reactions, there came a distinct change. With the attempts to eliminate obscurities and ambiguities of language, flamboyancy, and the frequently dominating prose rhythms, a more conversational, direct. and effective style of writing and speaking resulted. In 1900 he admonished that "as to style, seek only to be clear. Nothing else is important."

> Never try to be eloquent. Eloquence is the natural product of full knowledge, simple statement, deep feeling and ripe occasion—it comes spontaneously, and is not to be manufactured like a hat or a shovel.

We are advised to speak naturally. Speaking is "an intellectual performance, not a physical feat." Avoid pomposity. Pronounce the words distinctly. "Speak the speech; do not read it. . . ."

"Be careful of your appearance . . . the first impression which the audience gets should be an agreeable one." Don't hunger for their applause.

> Have no uneasiness that applause will not come; it will come if it is deserved, and no other kind is worth having. Clever marshaling of facts, clear and simple reasoning done with compactness and brevity, climaxes of

logic in the form of genuine appeal—
such phases of speech-making never
fail to produce hearty approval by an
audience. . . .

And finally, "be as brief as you are
simple, as plain as you are fair, and, content with a good job well done, stop when
you are through."

When students, frequently the most per-
ceptive textbook critics, responded enthusi-
astically to excerpts from this book which
had been distributed to them in class, I
suggested to the widow of Senator Beveridge reprinting the entire volume. Her
response was encouraging and she ex-
pressed the hope "to keep the little book
alive." The little book is, indeed, alive—and
well!

D. N. DIEDRICH
Ball State University
Muncie, Indiana

THE ART OF PUBLIC SPEAKING

THE ART OF
PUBLIC SPEAKING

THE first political speech I ever heard was typical of the oratory upon which most of us were brought up. Also it showed that, if he had lived, Abraham Lincoln might, perhaps, have been overthrown by the post-war politicians; for Lincoln's supreme idea was the reconstruction of the South on the basis of brotherhood and good-will— genuine reunion; whereas the rally-round-the-flag politicians wanted the South treated as a conquered province— genuine disunion.

So the words for which, above all others, the American people and the world now love and revere Lincoln, "with malice toward none, with charity for all . . . let us . . . bind up the Nation's wounds "— not only the wounds of the North, the East, the West, but the wounds of the whole Nation

—did not fit the plans of those who, for political purposes, wished to keep the war going long after it was over.

Therefore they fanned the embers of hatred. They kept old war passions alive, and even incubated new ones. Thus came a recrudescence of that emotional speech-making which in America was one after-effect of the French Revolution — speech-making which violates every principle of oratory, and which has done much to destroy that noble art in the United States.

The only Republicans in the county where we lived in my childhood were Union soldiers, among the most ardent of whom were my father and brothers; and when we had a political rally all of them came to the county seat, a little country town whose dirt streets were axle-deep with mud or ankle-deep with dust. On the edge of the village —for it was no more—was a grove of oak and walnut trees, where we Republicans

4

held our meetings. The Democrats held theirs a mile away on the other side of the county seat in a wood made up mostly of hickory trees.

OLD–TIME POLITICAL SPEECHES

IN the early seventies, when I was a very small boy, there was a Republican gathering in our Republican grove. The speaker was a well-known politician of the period and a typical post-war stump-speaker, who grew more furious at "the rebels" as the war receded in time.

Long, thick, inky-black hair flowed over his collar, and immense black mustaches added to his formidable and ferocious appearance. The August sun made the surrounding prairies shimmer with heat and even in the shade of the trees men mopped their brows, women fanned crying babies, and all were as uncomfortable as they were enthusiastic.

I sat between my parents on the front plank which, at either end and in the middle, rested on logs. The speaker, escorted by the committee, mounted the flag-draped platform, was introduced, threw off his coat and vest, tore his collar and tie from his neck, replaced them with a red bandanna handkerchief which made him look more militant than ever, ran his fingers through his mane and began:

"Comrades! And you, the mothers, wives, and sweethearts of my comrades! Who murdered our comrades? Rebels! Democrats!" (Tremendous cheering. A voice "Give 'm hell, John." More cheering.) "Who tried to shoot the Stars and Stripes from the heavens? Rebels! Democrats!" So the orator in a crimson torrent raged on, waving the flag, pounding the table, gesticulating wildly, shaking his head like an infuriated bull and working himself up to boiling heat, physically as well as emotionally. At last came a picturesque and blood-curdling climax.

It was a great speech everybody said, and so the little, barefoot boy believed it to be. After singing "Marching through Georgia," the farmers and their families got into their big wagons, some with fifers and drummers from out townships, and started homeward, hurrahing for our candidates. All were as happy as they were patriotic.

The very next week, under the protection of a Democratic farmer who lived near us, I went to a Democratic meeting in the hickory grove. We took our politics seriously and none of my family would attend; but I wanted so badly to hear the Democratic speech, that my parents finally consented, although with reluctance and misgiving.

As to violent delivery, exaggerated statement, and lack of argument, the Demo-

7

cratic speech was identical with the Republican speech I had heard a few days earlier — all was denunciation, only the thesis was reversed. We Republicans, it seemed, were rascals, scoundrels, and ought to be in jail, every last one of us. Again there was the acrobatic rage of the speaker, again the shedding of garments, again the lurid adjectives, again the senseless cheering, again the shouted encouragement from excited partisans to ''give 'm hell,'' again the general acclaim that it was a great speech, again the small-boy's acceptance that it was a great speech.

I was angered and mystified — how could we Republicans be such a bad lot? and, besides, had not our Republican speaker called these Democrats ''rebels''? It did not connect up, but, still, I was hot for my clan. However, it was a great speech; there could be no doubt about that outstanding fact. So was the verbal and emotional tempest, I had heard the week before, a great speech.

The greatness of these two speeches was the one thing upon which everybody agreed. The partisans of neither side repeated any arguments of either speaker — there were none to repeat—but there was ardent rivalry as to which speech was the greater. The word "great" was worked by everybody until the sweat of exhaustion poured from every letter of it.

Such were the performances that, for several decades after the Civil War, were called oratory. Even to-day we sometimes hear the same kind of public speaking, especially during political campaigns—the same furious delivery, the same extreme misstatement, the same unfairness, the same animosity, the same ignoring of fact and reason.

THE GREAT ARTISTS

Bur it is now fast disappearing, and it is to assist, however feebly, the restoration of the art of public speaking that I write these lines.

At this point it may, perhaps, be helpful to make mention of the circumstances which began to open my eyes, albeit dimly at first, to the errors of the "oratory" described. When I went to college, oratorical contests were in vogue; I needed the money and simply had to take the prizes. It was a matter of necessity rather than of ambition. I looked with freshman awe upon the college orators of the upper classes, but their methods seemed artificial and unconvincing. Country-bred youth though I was, I could see that; and other students, I found, thought the same.

Not until my senior year did we have a professor of oratory. I got no instruction or training until then, and had to think out for myself the elements of the subject. So, finally, I concluded that the basis of public speaking is this:

An audience is a composite person; therefore what will please, persuade, or convince an individual will do the same with a collection of individuals. The only difference is that since an audience is larger, tone and gesture should be stronger, but only enough stronger to fill the eye and ear of that composite person. From this idea flow the rules of the art of public speaking which I shall presently state.

Not until my twentieth year did I have an opportunity to hear a real orator, a master of the art; and that event confirmed the soundness of the theory set out above. In a Middle-Western town where I then chanced to be—I was a book agent that summer—Colonel Robert G. Ingersoll delivered one of his celebrated lectures. In every respect he was the reverse of the stump-speakers described at the beginning of this paper.

In the first place he was perfectly attired, freshly shaved, well groomed, neatly turned out in every particular. He came to the front of the platform in the most natural manner and, looking us in the eye in a friendly fashion, began to talk to us as if he were conversing with each of us personally.

He stood still, made no gestures for a long time, and when they came at last, they were, seemingly, so spontaneous and unstudied that we scarcely noticed them, so much a part of his spoken word did they appear to be. His gestures added to the force of his remarks. Only once did he show emotion, and then it was so appropriate, so obviously sincere, gestures so well expressing the physical reaction of his sentiments, that even this outburst was engaging.

In short, everything about Colonel Ingersoll was pleasing, nothing was repellent — a prime requisite to the winning of a cordial hearing from any audience big or little, rough or polite. Even the lilt of his rhetoric was made attractive; and be it said, in passing, that his blank-verse style was the only thing in the oratory of Colonel Ingersoll the good taste of which might, perhaps, be open to criticism.

At any rate, considered exclusively from the point of view of oratory as an art and without reference to his opinions, Ingersoll was one of the four greatest public speakers America has produced — that is, one of the four greatest artists. If we are to credit tradition, the others were Daniel Webster, Wendell Phillips, and Patrick Henry. Of course there have been many others, but these four are the outstanding masters.

In the case of Patrick Henry we deal with a genuine case of that misused and overworked word, "genius." By means of his natural gifts Henry supplied much that example and study can give, although it is certain that he bestowed a great deal of thought upon the subject and practiced more than it was supposed that he did.

SPEAKING AN ART

BEFORE taking up the basic rules, the observance of which constitutes the art of public speaking, we must get it firmly in mind, and bear it in mind all the time, that oratory is an art in the sense th t music, painting, sculpture, and the like are arts, or rather phases of art, since art is one and the same thing however manifested.

For art is the most finished expression of truth in its myriad aspects, with the least possible obstruction in that presentation, so that those who hear or look can get most clearly and easily the thing presented. It follows that art is the highest functioning of the mind and soul of man; and it follows,

14

too, that it requires the utmost instruction, training, and practice to become an artist of any kind.

Take music, for example : It would be a daring person who would undertake to play upon the piano or any musical instrument without having studied, not only that instrument, but the elements of music. If possible, singing is even harder. Or take acting. Years of practice after correct teaching are essential to the making of the accomplished actor — he or she who performs so well that the auditor is made to feel that all is natural and without effort. Was it not Emerson who said that a company of the poorest professionals is better than a company of the best amateurs?

Or painting ! — it would be absurd to attempt to produce a masterpiece on canvas without learning even the principles of drawing, to say nothing of having a knowledge of colors. But these essentials are

15

only the *a*, *b*'s of the education necessary to produce a good painting of any kind.

And so with any phase of art whatever. No sensible person would think of attempting it without information and training. For that matter shoeing a horse, driving an automobile, laying brick, keeping books, running a furrow, selling goods, and nearly everything requires knowledge and experience. Yet, curiously enough, most of us feel that we can practice without knowledge or effort the two oldest and noblest of the fine arts, writing and speaking.

For the purposes of this essay, the origin of this obsession, while interesting, is, perhaps, not important. It is enough to know that it is quite general. So, since public speaking is one of the two methods of shaping public opinion, let us look into the rules and principles of this art—rules and principles which the speaker must understand and obey as much as the musician, singer, actor, painter, or sculptor must understand and obey those of his or her art.

For public speaking is steadily becoming more important. New ideas are being advanced, some excellent, others unsound, the advocates of all striving to influence the public. The press does not and never can take the place of personal appeal — though justly influential, it is not decisive. So it is indispensable that leaders of opinion shall be able to state their views effectively by word of mouth.

This is especially true of legislators and executives, particularly the latter, since they must present policies and plans to the people, with clearness and force.

Of course one must have some natural aptitude for speaking, just as is the case with singing, painting, writing, salesmanship, inventing, or anything else. All the rules in the world and a lifetime of practice could not make a Fritz Kreisler into a Henry

17

Ford, an Edison into a Paderewski, or a Theodore Roosevelt into a John D. Rockefeller. But assuming natural endowment, knowledge and practice of the rules of the art are indispensable to the making of the finished orator.

Though ''the natural-born orator'' has advantages, any young man of average intelligence with uncommon industry and determination can become an acceptable public speaker. But he must study and work hard to gain that end. If he does so, however, and keeps everlastingly at it, he will, at last, do better than one who has oratorical gifts and does not improve them.

Shall we, then, consider what constitutes the art of public speaking?

MATTER

As to composition and structure of the speech, the rules of that art may be summarized thus:

Speak only when you have something to say.

Speak only what you believe to be true.

Prepare thoroughly.

Be clear.

Stick to your subject.

Be fair.

Be brief.

The maxims as to delivery can be stated more appropriately when we reach the discussion of that phase of speech-making. So let us now take up the rules just mentioned.

I

FAITH

First of all, then, speak only when you have something to say. Be sure that you

have a message to deliver. With reference
to your subject, let your feeling be that of
the inspired preacher, ''Woe is me if I
preach not the Gospel.'' Have ever in mind
Carlyle's dictum that nobody has a right
to speak in public unless he is so charged
with the subject, and the time and occasion
are so ripe for the hearing, that every word
will be fruitful of a deed—that is, con-
viction and action on the part of those who
listen.

This means, of course, utter sincerity.
Never under any circumstances or for any
reward tell an audience what you, yourself,
do not believe or are even indifferent about.
To do so is immoral and worse—it is to
be a public liar. Even from the lowest point
of view, to speak against convictions, or
without convictions, is fatal to the speaker.
Sooner or later the public ''gets on'' to the
situation and the speaker's influence is
impaired.

Thereafter people may go to hear such a person, but they do so only to be amused and entertained, not for instruction and guidance. To the hearers the speaker has become little more than a play-actor — perhaps not so much, indeed, since the actor performs for entertainment as an exhibition of art, whereas the speaker described sails under false colors and is neither orator nor actor.

Many years ago a distinguished speaker with rare oratorical gifts and thoroughly familiar with the mere technical rules of the art, lost his public influence because he was seldom in earnest and the idea of his insincerity became general. He was as inconstant as he was felicitous, had no principles, could argue on one side as ably as on the other, and often did argue on both sides of a given question. Moreover, he resorted to meretricious devices in delivery.

For example: Once in a campaign he

achieved a triumph before a great audience by answering aptly and well a difficult question put to him, during his speech, by a man who, seemingly, was merely one of his hearers. A commercial traveler who was present was so captivated that he went to hear the celebrated orator at a meeting some days later in another State; and at the same point in the same speech the same man asked the same question which was answered in the same way. It turned out that the questioner was the speaker's secretary. Other incidents of the kind became known, all illustrative of trickery.

The outcome of the whole matter — variableness, facility in wobbling, sensational devices — was that the public lost faith in this man's intellectual integrity, and, thereafter, people went to hear him only to be diverted.

Our campaign practices and the campaign requirements of party committees would do much harm in this respect, if the public were not aware that fulsome praise of party candidates and of prominent officials is purely conventional—a mere form of politeness, like "Good-morning," or, "How well you look." Still, the custom of delivering apostrophes to those in exalted positions or to heads of party tickets, regardless of the merits or deserts of the person thus verbally exalted, cannot be justified on any sensible or moral ground and ought to be abandoned.

The practice in high schools and colleges of appointing debating teams to support or oppose propositions, regardless of what the debaters believe, is questionable—indeed, bad, I think. It merely teaches intellectual dexterity while inducing moral indifference. Might it not be better to let students study the subject and select the side they believe to be right and sound? Is it not risky to ignore the ethical?

I would even carry this idea into the practice of the law. Of course it is hard to answer Lord Brougham's argument for the contrary — that every man is entitled to his day in court, has a right to be heard, and that the lawyer is only his mouthpiece. Perhaps the syllogism of that great English advocate cannot be overthrown as a matter of sheer logic. Nonetheless, all things considered, is it not better for an attorney to tell a client frankly that he is in the wrong and refuse to take his case if he insists upon litigation?

Being absolutely certain — and your heart and conscience will tell you — that you really have something to say to the public and that you must, positively must, tell your fellow citizens of the faith that is in you and the reasons therefor, next in order comes preparation. This is vital.

II

KNOWLEDGE

FIRST, last, and above all else, the public speaker is a teacher. The man or woman who presumes to talk to an audience should know more about the subject discussed than anybody and everybody in that audience. Otherwise, why speak at all? How dismal an uninformed speech! When coupled with sincerity, how pitiable! — and how poisonous! — for that very ingenuousness often causes the hearers to believe, for the time being, that the speaker knows what he is talking about.

Sincere ignorance is dangerous, until the public learns that the speaker is not well posted. All of us know of persons who are fervently honest and really eloquent so far as word arrangement and pleasing delivery go, but who have ceased to carry great weight with the public because, obviously, they have not broadly and deeply studied the subjects under public discussion. But until the people realize how uninformed and untrustworthy such persons are, they can do much harm.

So, the speaker must master his subject. That means that all facts must be collected, arranged, studied, digested — not only data on one side, but material on the other side and on every side — all of it. And be sure they are facts, not mere assumptions or unproved assertions. Take nothing for granted.

Therefore check up and reverify every item. This means painstaking research, to be sure, but what of it? — are you not proposing to inform, instruct, and advise your fellow citizens? Are you not setting yourself up as a teacher and counselor of the public?

Having assembled and marshaled the facts of any problem, think out for yourself the solution those facts compel. Thus your speech will have originality and personal force — it will be vital and compelling. There will be you in it. Then write out your ideas as clearly and logically as you can.

Until this point in your preparation is reached, do not read what others have written or said on the same thesis. If you do, it is likely that you will adopt their thought — indeed, this is almost certain unless you are blessed with an uncommonly strong, inquiring, and independent mind or cursed with an exceptionally stubborn, obstinate, and contentious mind.

But after the processes mentioned, nothing can be more helpful than to read everything on the subject that you can get hold of. Indeed, such comprehensive reading is invaluable. It is the best way to correct errors.

Also, of course, you must know what are

the arguments of those who do not agree with you. Besides, you may find that you are wholly wrong — in fact, you may learn that what you have believed to be a new idea that will compose all troubles and save the world, was exploded a thousand years before the time of Abraham.

The speech must now be rewritten — and then done over again, the oftener the better. The purpose of rewriting is to remove obscurities and ambiguities — in short, to make every statement logical and clear. It is said that, throughout his life, Lincoln would rewrite many times any proposition about which he was thinking in order to reduce the statement of that proposition to its simplest terms.

And condense, condense, condense. It is surprising how much can be cut out which, at first, seems to be indispensable. These superfluities add nothing to the argument and merely confuse the hearer. Bear in mind and apply to public speaking the meaning of the great von Moltke's final instructions to his officers at the beginning of the Franco-Prussian War: "Remember, gentlemen, that any order which can be misunderstood will be misunderstood."

In order to be lucid, study words — make that your hobby. You will find such study as engaging as it is useful. Though an old book, and one dealing with comparatively few words, Crabb's Synonyms is invaluable, because of the little essays about words, which essays are as charming as they are accurate. Other volumes in the same line will also be helpful.

The point to such research is to learn the exact shadings of the meaning of words to the end of making yourself understood. As everybody knows, many disputes arise from disagreements over the definition of terms employed in business contracts, political platforms, sectarian creeds, international treaties and "understandings," and the language of official personages.

Also ample knowledge of words does not increase but diminishes the vocabulary used by the public speaker, because words are thus well chosen and only for their effectiveness.

The final item of preparation is the submission of the finished manuscript to several friends for criticism and suggestion. Ask them to point out errors in statement of fact and weaknesses in reasoning. These critics should be of varied occupations and interests — an up-to-date business man, a labor leader or any informed workingman, a local politician, a well-posted woman, a high-school student, a sound scholar. Their comment is invaluable. Moreover, in this way are secured the views of a cross-section of the general public.

At last comes the ultimate revision,

tightening loose bolts, strengthening feeble places in argument, reinforcing statements of fact, making clearer points which some critic thinks obscure, and the like. Preparation thus finished, put aside your manuscript and make your speech.

Do not try to commit it to memory, unless it is to be delivered on a very important occasion and it is vital that the speech shall be reported accurately.

Some persons have a curious faculty for remembering the written word and it is easier for them to do so than to speak extemporaneously. It is said that Roscoe Conkling could repeat his manuscript verbatim after having read it but once or twice; and Emery A. Storrs was able, so it is reported, to reproduce a speech just as he had written it without reading it over again.

But such letter-perfect delivery is possible only to those of abnormal memories. Moreover, it is not desirable — it makes the speech rigid whereas it ought to be flexible.

The commanding reason for such thorough preparation is that the speaker shall become the master of his subject. Indeed, he should be able to answer almost any question that a hearer may ask him. It is, in fact, a good plan for the speaker, early in his address, to request anybody in the audience to rise and ask questions about matters not clear to the inquirer, provided the information is sought at the time the speaker is discussing that particular subject.

The answer should be given clearly and in good temper, and the questioner asked, in turn, whether he is satisfied. Have no fear that partisan opponents or contentious persons will make trick queries or impertinent interruptions for the purpose of confusing or embarrassing the speaker — that seldom happens, and when it does, the audience detects it and takes care of the situation.

There is nothing finer than the sense of fair play which animates an American audience when it feels that a speaker is sincere and informed and trying only to help the hearers to right conclusions. So keep in good humor, let nothing irritate you, depend upon the instinct, justice, and appreciation of your hearers.

The extensive preparation described is, of course, not necessary when you are already well informed on the subject to be discussed. Take a lawyer who has made a specialty of some particular branch of his profession, or a business man who knows his line from top to bottom, or a scientist with broad and exact information, or a preacher who keeps abreast of the times — such men have been preparing all their lives to speak informingly. Yet even they need to freshen themselves somewhat before undertaking to instruct their fellow citizens.

III

CLEARNESS

THE speech well in hand as to facts and argument, the manuscript out of mind — after all, the manuscript is only one stage in the process of producing the speech — the speaker takes the platform. Here comes the next rule, which, indeed, must be followed from first to last; but which can be stated more effectively at this point, perhaps, rather than earlier.

Make every sentence so plain that the dullest or most uninformed person in the audience cannot fail to understand the meaning of what is said. Have constantly in mind von Moltke's dictum that whatever *can* be misunderstood *will* be misunderstood. So use the simplest words that can express your thought and put them in such order that they do express your thought.

It is a good practice to pick out the least

intelligent-looking person in the audience and strive to make that person interested in your argument. This can be done only by lucid statement of fact and clear reasoning. An even better method is to center your talk on some small boy or girl present with parents.

Say to yourself — say out loud to your audience, if you like — that you will try to be so plain that the child will understand and remember your explanation of the question discussed, and after the meeting be able to tell what you have said.

This means, of course, that big or uncommon words must be avoided. Beware of adjectives — they are dangerous stimulants, to be used sparingly and with caution. Refrain from what is called rhetoric. Shun the ornate. Never try to be eloquent. Eloquence is the natural product of full knowledge, simple statement, deep feeling, and ripe occasion — it comes spontaneously, and is not to be manufactured like a hat or a shovel.

Too much emphasis cannot be put upon this rule of clearness, since, if you are not understood or are misunderstood, the purpose of the speech has failed — better not to have spoken at all. And, of course, you cannot expect others to get your meaning if you are not sure of it yourself. This takes us back to preparation, the completeness of which is basic.

But in the effort to be clear and plain, do not try to talk down to your audience. That is fatal. The loftiest theme can be treated best in simplest terms. Take, for example, the Sermon on the Mount, or, indeed, any of the teachings of Jesus, who, considered even from the human point of view, was the supreme master of the art of public address.

Or take Paul's speech to the Athenians on Mars' Hill, the finest example of oratory ever delivered by mortal man — or, not far below Paul's masterpiece, that of Lincoln at Gettysburg. These sermons and speeches were exalted, yet they were in the language of the common people.

So pitch your speech on the highest plane. The heart and mind of the humblest man yearn for better and nobler things and the mass instinct and intellect tend upward.

After a notable success at a big meeting in one of our great cities, the speaker was asked whether he made that kind of a speech to country gatherings.

"I try to make a better one," he answered.

"But are you not afraid you will talk over the heads of your audience?"

"No," said he. "I have spoken at crossroads, in barns and blacksmith shops, and never yet have I faced an American audience that I felt that I could talk up to —

that is, the audience always has impressed me as really wanting something higher and finer than I am able to give them.''

To the supreme end of being understood, stick to the subject. Do not go off on side-issues. Digression is perilous. It distracts attention which is hard to recover and sometimes never is recovered. Side-remarks may be diverting, but are obstacles in the current of the argument.

IV

HUMOR

UNLESS you are naturally witty and have a gift for story-telling, do not try to be funny or to tell an anecdote. Few things are more distressing and even painful than such attempts at humor by one who cannot carry it off well. Even those who have that entertaining faculty should employ it rarely and with discretion.

Long ago in a State in the Mississippi

Valley, a leading lawyer was also our Republican "Keynoter" at the beginning of campaigns. He was able, a master of logic, and loved statistics. His one defect was that he had no more humor than a stone. To remedy this, friends urged that he tell some funny stories. He grumbled, but agreed at last. However, he knew no such stories. So we collected several for him.

Then came the big meeting where, during his speech, he was to tell them. It was held in the Court-House yard of a county seat. It was an old-fashioned political rally, and the "paramount issue" was the tariff. Thousands attended, nearly all farmers. Our hero poured figures and argument upon his audience for an hour or two, forgetting entirely his stories. At last a friend pulled his coat-tails and reminded him of his neglected humor.

"Oh, yes," said he, and turning to the crowd remarked with a grimace meant to be a pleasant smile, but more expressive of disgust:

"Now, ladies and gentlemen, I will tell you some funny stories which my friends have collected for me."

And he told them — for half an hour he told them, one after another. Not a laugh from the assembled multitude, not a smile. It was ghastly. Having finished, he laid down his notes — he could not remember the stories without notes — and, with a sigh of relief, said:

"Now, ladies and gentlemen, I'll go on with my argument. As I was saying when I had to stop and tell those darned stories . . ."

The audience, with open mouths, wondered what it had all been about. Thereafter nobody ever made mention to that great lawyer of the circumstance or asked him to tell a story or make a joke.

The late Jonathan P. Dolliver, a most

captivating speaker and powerful debater, was so prolific in genuine fun that he kept vigilant watch over himself in this regard — only a very few of the enchanting drolleries that bubbled from him in private conversation ever got into his public utterances. These few are famous; such, for example, as his one-line description of the ineptitude of an opponent, "like a man emptying a barrel of coal ashes in a high wind."

But able public men who could crack jokes effectively and tell amusing stories delightfully, and who gave rein to their disposition, have ruined their reputations for statesmanship by thus acquiring reputations as wits and humorists. S. S. Cox, of New York — "Sunset" Cox, as he was called — is a notable example; in later life this capable statesman bewailed his facility as a fun-maker and said that it had checked his political progress, which, undoubtedly, was the case.

41

Lincoln was prudent in the extreme in this regard — notwithstanding his gift of humor and his skill in story-telling, you will find scarcely a trace of them in his debates with Douglas and not the faintest gleam in his Cooper Union Speech or other historic addresses.

It is related of Oliver P. Morton, who had a remarkable aptitude for remark and narration that would send audiences into gales of laughter, that after he had thus affected a political State Convention he told his friends in despair that he feared he had ruined his future, but that if he could live down that funny speech, he never would tell another story or perpetrate another witticism in a public address as long as he lived. And he never did.

After all, such things are admissions by the speaker that he cannot hold his audience by facts and reason, but must rest and amuse them by the comic and grotesque.

When a story must be told, make it brief; not over one minute at the very outside.

And, unless you cannot control your enjoyment of your wit, do not laugh or chuckle over your own jokes — to do so is as if you should stop and clap your hands at what you think one of your eloquent passages.

This does not mean that you should be stolid and dry as dust. Quite the contrary. In oratory as in conversation dullness is one of the unpardonable sins. It is not necessary to be heavy in order to be informed. So let your remarks be bright and pointed. In fact, the audience wants nothing of the speaker so much as that he shall get to the point. We remember the advice of a veteran on the platform to an aspiring young orator: "If you don't strike oil in two minutes, stop boring."

Above all things, keep unction out of

your speech. Indulge in no holier-than-thou appeals. Pleas for "righteousness" have so often been made by mountebanks that all of us have come to suspect the users of such verbal sanctimoniousness. You can take many risks, but you cannot hazard doubt of your good faith.

V

FAIRNESS

OF even greater importance, if possible, than the rule of clearness and simplicity is that of fairness. The speaker must be so just that his strongest opponent will admit that he is fair. State the other side as well as its ablest advocate could present it, and then give your reasons against it.

Then tell what you stand for, and advance the facts and reasons in support of your position. What you are trying to do and all you ought to do is to instruct those who have not mastered the subject as you have done and to convince them that your opponents are wrong and you are right.

So never misrepresent your opponent — even the exigencies of "politics" do not justify falsehood. Make your statement of his position so just and unbiased that even he will concede your fairness.

Personalities have no place in the speech of a gentleman — and always you must be that, a matter I shall say more about when I consider the rules of delivery. So avoid personalities — at best they are cheap, and, besides, the use of them gives your audience the impression that you are prejudiced. When that happens, you have lost an asset.

For the same reason denounce only when there is real and blazing cause for such scourging, which seldom is the case. Abuse and vituperation are indefensible except in rare instances. Also they are the most dangerous weapons in the arsenal of oratory, poisoned daggers which usually wound and infect those who wield them.

For the most part your attitude should be that of kindliness — not an assumed kindliness which is mere hypocrisy, but genuine kindliness that flows from a friendly heart. After all, most people mean well, and you ought to feel toward them and speak to them accordingly.

Strong, good, and able public men of a certain temperament frequently impair their usefulness by assuming that all who do not agree with them are scoundrels. Their souls have soured, and, with malice toward all and charity for none, vilification of opponents becomes habitual. But see what an error it is, even as a matter of art! — do we not instinctively turn away from the suspicious, vindictive person of ill-feeling and bitter speech?

All this does not mean that the public speaker shall be a flabby sentimentalist, uttering milk-and-water platitudes. Far from it. Be practical, be pointed, let your blade be bright and have a keen edge — only do not dull and stain it with animosity. Even so, I would rather hear a speech with some acid in it than one so pious and unnaturally " good " that it is not human — such talk always makes me feel that lukewarm, diluted treacle is being poured over me.

Sometimes, to be sure, though not often, denunciation is needed. When it is needed, strike and spare not. Call a spade a spade, and name names. But let the fire of your assault be made hotter by regret and reluctance that facts and the public interest compel your burning words — only do not say that you are sorry that you must so speak, for your audience will see it if you really feel it.

Not long ago a man of discernment told me that the radio will destroy public speaking; for, said he, " we listened in the other night and heard the speeches at a great banquet. They were on taxation; and they sounded very thin — few points, little argument, facts rare, words numerous.''

But does not that prove that the radio will help restore oratory, since the public will demand facts and reasons well and briefly stated, will tolerate only real eloquence, and will reject in disgust banal sentiment and wordy emptiness?

The after-dinner speech is now recognized as a branch of oratory; but, generally speaking, it is, rather, a form of entertainment. At such times we tolerate and even enjoy '' flights of eloquence '' and humorous burlesques which would not impress us on important occasions. Still, even in banquet oratory, all is not trifling, and a speaker with a message may, perhaps, without offense to hearers or disadvantage to himself or herself, heed the rules herein stated. Some after-dinner speeches that have found places in literature have been the result of just such processes.

Of course the highest of rostrums for the uttering of noblest truths is the Pulpit. Since, as a rule, preachers have given their lives to study, they need only to keep up-to-date in science, theology, philosophy, and general literature to write sermons rich in wisdom and helpfulness. Indeed, most of them do — the best public addresses of the last fifty years and to-day were and are made by preachers. Take, for example, Beecher, Simpson, Lorimer, Brooks, and others of only slightly lesser stature.

Where many preachers are deficient is in delivery. Fine sermons are often ruined by Bible-thumping, machine-gun utterance, and other offensivenesses.

DELIVERY

LET us now examine the question of delivery — it is barely second in importance to the matter of the address, since your remarks must be spoken well and agreeably in order to reach and impress the hearers, or even to be understood by them.

The rules of delivery may be indexed thus:

Speak quietly and naturally.

Be serene and never pompous.

Enunciate distinctly.

Control emotion — never get excited.

Dress well; neither negligently nor with ostentation.

Suppress the craving for applause.

Stop when you are through.

To enlarge upon these briefly:

I

COMPOSURE

To begin with, stand still, at least for a while. It is better not to move about at all; but, if you cannot remain in the same place during your address, do so until the audience gets used to you and until you have shown your serenity, your mastery of yourself.

Speak slowly, especially when beginning, but only slowly enough to make your words understood. This does not mean to drag out your syllables — that is painful to your hearers. I have listened to speakers who separated words so much that only by close attention could the connection between them be realized.

On the other hand, refrain from rapid speaking. When words tumble over one another, the meaning of sentences is lost in a jungle of articulation. Your purpose is to make yourself understood — remember all the time that ruling idea.

Let your first words be conversational, quite as if you were talking to a friend. Indeed, the whole speech should be made in that tone and manner, unless genuine feeling compels you to speak more loudly and with greater physical force. But keep a stiff bit on that same emotion — yield to it when you feel you must, but never let it get the upper hand of you.

The speech is supposed to be an intellectual performance, not a physical feat. You are a teacher, not an acrobat; an artist, not a dervish.

Elbert Hubbard, when a boy of twelve, heard Wendell Phillips, and thus describes him and his manner of speaking:

"One man arose and spoke. He lifted his hands, raised his voice, stamped his foot, and I thought he was a very great man. He was just introducing the Real Speaker.

"Then the Real Speaker walked slowly down to the front of the stage and stood very still. And everybody was also quiet . . . Phillips just stood there and told us about" the lost arts; "he stood still with one hand behind him or resting on his hip or at his side and the other hand motioned a little — that was all.

"We expected every minute that he would burst out and make a speech, but he did not — he just talked . . . and I understood it all.

"I remember the presence and attitude of the man as though it were but yesterday. The calm courage, deliberation, beauty and strength of the speaker — his knowledge, his gentleness, his friendliness! I had heard many sermons, and some had terrified me.

"This time I had expected to be thrilled too. . . . And here it was all just quiet joy — I understood it all. I was pleased with myself; and being pleased with myself I was pleased with the speaker. He was the biggest and best man I had ever seen — the first real man.''

There is your model. No prancing about, no striding to and fro like a caged and hungry lion, no stamping of foot or pounding with fist or shaking the same at high heaven, no tossing of arms as if in agony or rage, no shouting or bellowing nor yet tremolo tones and whispering; especially no grimacing or facial contortions.

Merely be quiet and at ease and talk like a human being — a friendly person conversing with friends, a kindly but intelligent teacher telling with clearness and force what you have to say.

But though cordial, do not be familiar with your audience. Nothing is more offensive to sensible men and women than the ''folksy-folk'' manner and bearing of a speaker — they know that such things are assumed for a purpose.

Audiences resent over-friendliness and sometimes rebuke it openly. One such instance in a certain State in the north Mississippi Valley became a standing joke for more than a decade and all but shattered the ambitions of the offender. He was an "orator" of the early post-war period and was as patronizing as he was violent.

In a town where he was generally disliked, he began his speech by saying how it warmed the cockles of his heart to again meet and address so many dear, dear friends —and he enlarged upon his affection for those present. How he loved them, his precious friends!

"Name one,——!" (calling the speaker's name) "Name one!" shouted a tall, lank countryman, rising in the audience and pointing a long bony finger at the orator.

A gale of loud and derisive laughter swept the crowd; the speaker could not go on, and the meeting broke up.

Even had there been no personal antagonism to the speaker, he had broken a rule of fundamental politeness — he had presumed upon his audience. He had patronized his hearers, been over-familiar, struck too coarsely the chord of amity—a thing that "is not done," as the English say, even when intimacy exists, which it did not in this case.

So indulge in no extreme expressions of regard for your hearers. Make no show of affection. Just be considerate, respectful, friendly in natural and genuine fashion.

From first to last, face your main audience. Never turn about and address the chairman of the meeting, for example. When you do, the great body of your hearers lose your point, and sometimes become restless and irritated. Keep control of those in front of you, which can be done only by looking them in the eye all the time and speaking to them directly.

57

II

ENUNCIATION

It is not necessary to shout in order to be heard. Perfect enunciation will carry your words farther than all the roaring and straining of vocal chords you can do, will carry them. Pronounce every word distinctly and separately; do not slur them or run them together. Do not let your voice fall to nothingness at the end of a sentence, since this usually results in the audience not hearing the last word and thus losing the meaning of the sentence.

Words and sentences should be spoken neatly, not snapped off, nor even clipped, mind you, but neatly and with precision. The whole purpose is to make yourself heard and understood. Speaking in an ordinary conversational tone, Wendell Phillips could reach thousands. So could Ingersoll. Yet both had gentle voices. Correct enunciation solves the problem of how to make one's self heard at long distances.

Shakespeare said the best thing about delivery that ever has been said by anybody, just as he said the best things on most subjects of permanent importance. Hamlet's instruction to the players he had employed is, of course, familiar to all; but it fits in so well here that I venture to reproduce it:

"Speak the speech . . . trippingly on the tongue; but if you mouth it . . . I had as lief the town-crier spoke my lines. Nor do not saw the air too much with your hand . . . but use all gently; for in the very torrent, tempest, and, as I may say, the whirlwind of passion, you must acquire and beget a temperance that may give it smoothness.

"Oh, it offends me to the soul to see a robustious . . . fellow tear a passion to tatters, to very rags, to split the ears of the groundlings. . . .

59

"Be not too tame, neither, but let your own discretion be your tutor. Suit the action to the word, the word to the action; with this special observance, that you o'erstep not the modesty of nature. . . . Overdone . . . though it make the unskilful laugh, cannot but make the judicious grieve."

III

MASTERY

By being the master of your subject and of yourself, be the master of your audience. But that dominance cannot be yours if you are uncertain and ill-prepared. Dignity and power come from full knowledge, deep thought, and sure faith as well as from personality. No wonder that the common people heard Jesus gladly, "for he taught them as one having authority."

Speak your speech; do not read it — to read it proves either that you have not mastered your subject or that you cannot remember your manuscript, or both. Even Presidential speeches when read are tiresome. Much better talk by radio — time and expense of hearers would be saved thereby. Also those who listen in would not be bored.

IV

APPEARANCE

BE careful of your appearance. That is the highest compliment you can pay to your audience. Let everything about you be neat and attractive. Dress well. See that collar and shirt are fresh, shoes polished, hair trimmed — in short, look to every detail of your grooming. The reason is that the first impression which the audience gets of the speaker should be an agreeable one.

The idea is the same as that which forbids the use of uncouth or florid language or the making of digressions or the doing of anything which will interfere with getting the message to the mind and heart of the hearer. In like manner, the appearance of the speaker should be such as not to distract attention from what he says.

Speakers of the first class always have taken much pains in this matter. I have made mention of the correct and pleasing attire of Ingersoll when delivering a public address. If possible that of Wendell Phillips was even more agreeable. Webster came near carrying the matter of dress and personal appearance to the extreme — fortunately, he stopped just short of it. But William Pinkney, the foremost lawyer of his time, did not; he overdressed, which is well-nigh more offensive than negligence of attire. Roscoe Conkling wore clothes so striking as to be noted and cause remark — the very thing to be avoided.

V

APPLAUSE

I HAVE known more speakers of rare aptitude spoiled by the desire for applause and efforts to win it than by any other error. So avoid such things. Of course, all of us like and want appreciation, and the applause of an audience is sweet; but it is intoxicating, too, and in that alluring fact is the danger.

For example, a speaker who measures his success by handclapping and cheers wants to arouse such demonstrations as soon as he can and as often as possible. So, early in his speech, he makes some extreme or "catchy" assertion which his heated partisans or personal followers promptly applaud. This stimulates him, and, to get and give another thrill, he soon says something still more extravagant which brings louder acclaim.

63

Thus, by action and reaction between speaker and audience, both get into a state of mind altogether unworthy and well-nigh unintelligent. Nobody is benefited, nobody instructed, nobody convinced. To be sure, partisans are pleased, but the speaker had them on his side already; the open-minded, however, are disgusted, perhaps offended, and it is they who should have been won over.

Of course applause there must be, the more of it the better — but it must come naturally and spontaneously, as the result of well-made, convincing argument and appropriate, heartfelt appeal, and never in partisan response to exaggerations worked in for the purpose of getting such outbursts.

Have no uneasiness that applause will not come; it will come if it is deserved, and no other kind is worth having. Clever marshaling of facts, clear and simple reasoning done with compactness and brevity,

climaxes of logic in the form of genuine
appeal — such phases of speech-making
never fail to produce hearty approval by an
audience and even by hearers who, at first,
were inclined to disagree with the speaker's
point of view.

Fear not that your speech will lack fire.
If you mean what you say, fervor will
come naturally and with effectiveness. The
fact that you are in earnest will give force
and vigor to your delivery. But control
your intentness — do not let it control you.

Speak with spirit, of course; vapid
delivery is unattractive, even repellent.
Merely see to it that yours is a disciplined
ardor and that your passion does not run
away with you.

Although a vague way of putting it, perhaps, counsel as to delivery can best be
summed up by saying that the bearing,
words, and tones of the speaker should
be those of a gentleman — that mingling

of consideration for others, self-respect, kindliness, and dignity. Though impossible of exact description, there is nothing which an audience senses so quickly as this spiritual and intellectual quality of a speaker or the lack of it.

VI

BREVITY

AND now the final rule and of all rules the hardest to observe: Stop when you are through. Often the favorable effect on an audience of a really good speech is impaired by the speaker going on and on after he has made his case. Some speakers appear unable to make an end — as William M. Evarts said of his long sentences, "they lack terminal facilities."

So the audience is tired out, becomes bored, and the points already scored by the speaker are dulled by the masses of verbiage thereafter flung at his hearers.

To keep a speech within reasonable length but one subject should be treated. The campaign requirement of dealing with every current question as well as with the achievements or deficiencies of an administration and laudation of candidates, makes impossible adequate discussion of anything except by taking an intolerable length of time.

All enduring speeches have been comparatively short. None of the sermons of Jesus could, by any possibility, have occupied three quarters of an hour, and most of them must have been less than half as long. It is curious how perfectly His familiar talks fit the scientific theory of the university lecture.

During the seventeenth century the university custom became general of limiting lectures to one hour. More than two hundred years ago professors in German universities, for purely practical reasons, shortened the lecture to forty-five minutes.

Within the last thirty-five years, it was demonstrated that this limit is a scientific one, for Dr. Leo Bürgerstein, of Vienna, proved that, except under extraordinary circumstances, attention begins to lag after three quarters of an hour — this even with the young, fresh, eager minds of students. With miscellaneous audiences the risk of speaking for a longer time is, of course, much greater. Remember also that it is hard for any but an uncommonly vigorous and retentive intellect to grasp more than a very few ideas at one time.

So be as brief as you are simple, as plain as you are fair, and, content with a good job well done, stop when you are through.

THE END